Entrepreneurial Behavior:

Transforming an Innovative Idea into an Entrepreneurial Product

An Open Textbook Adaptation by Textbook Equity

Published and Distributed by

Textbook Equity, Inc.

Fearlessly Copy, Distribute, Remix™
opencollegetextbooks.org

Table of Contents

I have not failed. I've just found 10,000 ways that won't work.
- Thomas Edison

Introduction

There are literally dozens and dozens of different definitions of 'the entrepreneur' and the concept of 'entrepreneurship'. Researchers and writers often seem to pick the definition that best fits the area they are discussing. We have explicitly linked entrepreneurship to the capability for exploiting successfully innovative ideas in a commercially competitive market. Leaving to one side the fact that individuals working in the public and non-profit sectors can be very enterprising, in historic and policy making terms entrepreneurship refers to business behavior related to innovation and growth. For our purposes, entrepreneurs may be broadly defined as people who manage a business with the intention of expanding that business by applying some form of innovation and with the leadership and managerial capacity for achieving their goals, generally in the face of strong competition from other firms, large and small. The overall aim of this book, therefore, is to provide you with opportunities to consider and reflect on the personal aspects involved in transforming an innovative idea into an entrepreneurial product.

LEARNING OUTCOMES

After studying this book you should

- Understand the nature of entrepreneurship

- Understand the function of the entrepreneur in the successful, commercial application of innovations

- Confirm your entrepreneurial business idea

- Identify personal attributes that enable best use of entrepreneurial opportunities

- Explore entrepreneurial leadership and management style

- Identify the requirements for building an appropriate entrepreneurial team

1. Economic Function of the Entrepreneur

Broadly, entrepreneurs have two vital roles to play in the economy: (1) to introduce new ideas and, (2) to energize business processes. Strictly speaking, the term entrepreneur, which derives from the French words entre (between) and prendre (to take), referred to someone who acted as an intermediary in undertaking to do something. The term was originally used to describe the activities of what today we might call an impresario, a promoter or a deal maker. The entrepreneur first made an appearance as a distinct economic concept in France, twenty years before the 'father' of economics, Adam Smith, published his Wealth of Nations in 1776. Richard Cantillon, an Irishman living in France, suggested in 1756 that the entrepreneur was someone prepared to bear uncertainty in engaging in risky arbitrage, buying goods and services at a certain (fixed) price in one market to be sold elsewhere or at another time for uncertain future prices, usually in other market (though, throughout economic history, hoarders or traders who try to 'corner' a market have sought super-profits in the same markets when short supplies send prices rocketing upwards). This concept of entrepreneur as arbitrager is still relevant today but was clearly influenced by the dominance at that time of trade as the chief means for accumulating new wealth and capital. Manufacturing and trade dominated Britain's heyday in Victorian times whereas today, as the case studies show, it is technology, knowledge and services that provide most, though by no means all, entrepreneurial opportunities. In other words, entrepreneurship exists in its context as Illustration 1.

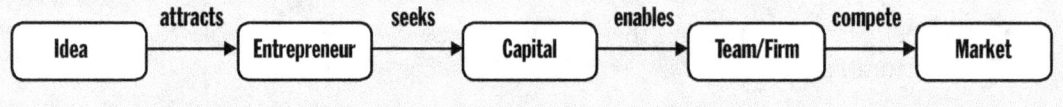

Illustration 1. Business Competition Chain

Here, the role of the entrepreneur is to conceive a business idea in terms of an innovation to be brought successfully to the market and to find the wherewithal to make this happen. The entrepreneur does not necessarily need to have the design, production or delivery skills (this is the function of the firm) nor to shoulder all or most of the risk (this is often assumed by the providers of finance or investors). Indeed, the notion of the entrepreneur as a risk-taking trader began to be challenged early on by the view of the entrepreneur as an adventurous self-employed manager capable of combining, to personal advantage, capital and labor. It is interesting to note that in France today the entrepreneur is a more generic term mainly referring to small property developers and owners of small construction firms. It would be wrong to state that the element of risk-bearing has completely disappeared from the modern concept of the entrepreneur. The successful management of risk is an important entrepreneurial attribute. However, it does seem true that a swift perception of opportunities and the ability to coordinate the activities of others emerge as the more central economic skills of the modern entrepreneur.

Austrian economist Joseph Schumpeter (1934), who has had a seminal influence on entrepreneurship, as well as innovation, placed the entrepreneur at the center of his theory of economic development. Schumpeter defined the entrepreneur simply as someone who acts as an agent of change by bringing into existence a 'new combination of the means of production'. New combinations include process, product and organizational innovations. The means of production includes capital, equipment, premises, raw materials, labor and, in recent times, information. Currently, knowledge has been added to the list as the indispensable ingredient for business success in the new millennium.

The essence of Schumpeter's approach is that entrepreneurs are competitive and always strive to gain an edge over their competitors. When they begin to consolidate and slow down, they revert to being ordinary managers and, in Schumpeter's terms, are no longer entrepreneurial. Thus attitudes to growth and the actual attainment of growth are essential elements of the concept of entrepreneurship. The attainment part of the concept, of course, implies a high level of managerial competence in all the five stages in Illustration 1 and a high competence in social and commercial interactions outside the firm with other firms, regulators and, above all, customers and consumers. This implies that entrepreneurial firms that innovate successfully and encourage new innovations are likely to be different from most other firms. They appear to be more open and supportive of different opinions and ideas. If you are developing your own idea as part of an organization (or if you feel that your idea will need the combined efforts of a firm for its implementation), Assessment 1 below will help you identify where you need to develop and negotiate support both inside and outside the firm. The art of negotiation is a key entrepreneurial skill.

The characteristics of entrepreneurial firms that are successful at launching innovations have been widely studied and are reflected in the questions asked in Assessment 1. The checklist should serve as a useful tool for gauging the innovative support from your current situation and as a guideline for the sort of atmosphere that needs to develop in a firm in order to maximize its entrepreneurial potential. When faced with very real resource constraints, maintaining motivation to set up and run such a firm can be very tough. The main motivation for entrepreneurs to overcome the barriers of economic pressure and uncertainty, according to Schumpeter (who was writing in the 1930s), were the prospects of upward social mobility into the capitalist class. At the start of the 21st century, with the almost universal dominance of market-based economic

Assessment 1. Characteristics of the Entrepreneurial Firm Checklist

Referring to the characteristics of successful innovation, complete the characteristics of the entrepreneurial firm checklist. Consider the ideal firm for bringing your idea to market (or if your ideas have not yet crystallized, an enterprising group or firm of at least two other people you know). Make a note about the purpose of the firm or team before you answer the questions. If the answer is 'Yes' write a brief example. If the answer is 'No', write the main reason.

Yes   No

❑   ❑   **1. Does the firm have strong confidence in its technical capabilities and knowledge?** An entrepreneurial firm has to have within it a proper working knowledge of the core technical and business processes used by successful firms in the sector and, especially the technologies and business processes that are the source of its competitive strengths. It is generally dangerous to outsource these core capabilities unless the real innovation is organizational or marketing.

_____

❑   ❑   **2. Is there a strongly shared culture and value system?** A strong sense of belonging and clear values are defining features of most entrepreneurial firms, which are often very explicit in their efforts to construct a living culture in the firm based on the shared values and positive mental attitudes.

_____

❑   ❑   **3. Does a strong policy of internal communication, transparency, and sharing of knowledge form a central part of the culture?** Successful business people work continuously and hard at improving their ability to communicate clearly and effectively; successful firms understand that innovations and motivation come from fostering internal sharing of information and knowledge.

_____

☐   ☐   **4. Are all members of staff aware of and share a sense of mission to achieve the firm's overall strategic aims?** A strong sense of shared purpose in relation to the firm's strategic aims and collective pride and determination in achieving those aims is a strong sign of an entrepreneurial culture in a firm.

_____

☐   ☐   **5. Is there a strong customer focus?** Judging customer tastes and needs is fundamental not only to entrepreneurial success but also to developing an innovative internal culture and achieving a self-managing total quality assurance system. In larger firms an important part of the system to support this is having special customer liaison or account executives to champion the customer's point of view, but in successful small firms all responsible members of the firm take on this role.

_____

☐   ☐   **6. Is there follow up on commitments and customer feedback?** Demonstrating persistence in sticking to commitments and, especially, in responding to customer feedback (good and bad) leads to a strong reputation for reliability and trustworthiness (the key attributes of high quality in the eyes of other businesses and customers.)

_____

☐   ☐   **7. Is public recognition given to customer and staff successes?** The best way to foster a team spirit and sense of belonging not only for staff but for key customers as well is to conduct employee, contractor, and customer appreciation activities whenever a suitable opportunity arises (including press releases if appropriate) and, in any case, have regular events throughout the year to celebrate achievements.

_____

☐   ☐   **8. Does the firm have a system for monitoring trends and changes in its markets?** In some firms, employee teams are charged with identifying STEEP, market and production factors that can have direct and indirect effects on their product lines while monitoring emerging technologies to find new ways of applying them to their products.

☐   ☐   **9. Does the firm have a system for objectively evaluating market changes and trends and identifying emergent opportunities?** Entrepreneurial firms are ahead of the herd so try to make things happen, rather than react to outside developments. but their business success depends on their ability to determine accurately and realistically the risk's prospects for success.

☐   ☐   **10. Is development and project work carried out in cross-functional teams?** Most entrepreneurial firms make use of cross-functional teams (teams composed, say, of designers, production and marketing people) to manage key projects and to develop new innovative products.

---

systems and a hugely increased middle class, the need to cope with the direct and indirect threats of 'globalization' is now often cited as the spur to innovation. For others, economic survival or the chance to create something of value are the driving motivators. Whatever the personal ambitions of entrepreneurial small firm owners, their role in introducing innovations and in improving overall economic development and efficiency is important.

Basically, the concept of development from an economic viewpoint means the growth of goods and services in an economy usually measured in total or per capita rates of growth in all goods and services, known as the Gross Domestic Product (GDP) or the Gross National Product (GNP) when nationally owned overseas goods and services are included. In advanced industrial economies such as Britain, France, Germany and so on, policy objectives tend to be targeted on improving economic performance rather than development per se. As an alternative to an economic approach, one of the best known psychologically-based economic development models that is still very influential, David McClelland's achievement motivation model, pays less attention to structural factors while the psychological determinants of economic behavior are more strongly emphasized:

> *Some wealth or leisure may be essential to development in other fields the arts, politics, science, or war but we need not insist on it. However, the question why some countries develop rapidly in the economic sphere at certain times and not at others is in itself of great interest, whatever its relation to other types of cultural growth. Usually, rapid economic growth has been explained in terms of 'external' factors favorable opportunities for trade, unusual natural resources, or conquests that have opened up new markets or produced internal political stability. But I am interested in the internal factors in the values and motives men have that lead them to exploit opportunities, to take advantage of favorable trade conditions; in short, to shape their own destiny.- (McClelland 1968, p. 74)*

McClelland's preferred entrepreneurial motivator, the need for achievement or nAch as it is usually abbreviated – 'a desire to do well, not so much for the sake of social recognition or prestige, but to attain an inner feeling of personal accomplishment' – is a more psychologically-based theory. McClelland himself summarized an alternative economic development theory as 'a society with a generally high level of nAch will produce more energetic entrepreneurs who, in turn, produce more rapid economic development'. However, McClelland was quite disparaging about the profit motive as the mainspring of entrepreneurial activity:

> *Since businessmen had obviously shifted their concern from intrinsic worth to money worth, Marx and other economists endowed man with a psychological characteristic known as the 'profit motive'. The capitalist, at any rate, was*

pictured as being driven by greed, by the necessity of making money or keeping up his rate of profit.

That such an assumption is a typical oversimplification of rational or armchair psychology has recently begun to be realized by historians in particular who have studied the lives of actual business entrepreneurs in the nineteenth century. Oddly enough, many of these men did not seem to be motivated by a desire for money as such or by what it would buy.– (McClelland 1961, p. 233)

"Wall Street" (1987) Gordon Gekko: Address to Teldar Paper Stockholders

- Teldar Paper has 33 different vice presidents, each earning over $200,000 a year. Now, I have spent the last two months analyzing what all these guys do, and I still can't figure it out. One thing I do know is that our paper company lost $110 million last year, and I'll bet that half of that was spent in all the paperwork going back and forth between all these vice presidents.

- The new law of evolution in corporate America seems to be survival of the unfittest. Well, in my book you either do it right or you get eliminated.

- In the last seven deals that I've been involved with, there were 2.5 million stockholders who have made a pre-tax profit of $12 billion. Thank you.

- I am not a destroyer of companies. I am a liberator of them!

- The point is, ladies and gentleman, is that greed – for lack of a better word – is good.

- Greed is right.

- Greed works.

- Greed clarifies, cuts through, and captures the essence of the evolutionary spirit.

- Greed, in all of its forms – greed for life, for money, for love, knowledge – has marked the upward surge of mankind.

Assessment 2. Motivation for Entrepreneurial Behavior

☐ 1. Do you think that profit maximization is the main motivation to entrepreneurial behavior?

☐ 2. Does profit have to be the main motivation of a successful business owner?

☐ 3. What alternatives or additional motives can you identify?

Clearly, the 'oversimplification' of the profit motive determining economic development has survived longer than McClelland believed it would and remains a central pillar to current business and economic analysis. Other motives include the need for autonomy, to 'be my own boss', to support a preferred lifestyle, to provide security for the family, to achieve social status and so on. Nevertheless, earning profits and making money also feature as important motives and the potential profitability of a new product is still usually the acid test of its likely viability. And well know entrepreneurs to the press and public are usually very successful and very rich business owners.

2. Entrepreneurial Qualities

It is now widely accepted that, apart from the start up phase, most small firms in Europe are more concerned about survival rather than growth and relatively few are especially entrepreneurial (Gray 1998). Consequently, a lot of research in this field has focused on finding the characteristics that set entrepreneurs and their firms apart from others. Elizabeth Chell (1985, 1999), a social psychologist, has examined numerous psychological trait-based approaches and concluded that, whilst psychological aspects such as 'entrepreneurial intention' and the 'ability to recognize opportunities' are strongly linked to entrepreneurial behavior, the context in which the entrepreneur operates is also very important. Entrepreneurship reflects complex interactions between the individual and the situation, which has to be dynamic because business situations are always changing.

Perceptions and judgment are, therefore, key elements in this process. Indeed, more than 20 years ago, Mark Casson (1982) identified 'judgment' as one of the qualities that distinguishes the successful entrepreneur from the much larger group of non-entrepreneurial SME owners. As mentioned before, business judgment can reflect an innate ability but most frequently it directly derives from experience (or, more accurately, learning from experience). However, past experience can also filter out our ability to spot new opportunities or threats. Cultural effects related to family, locality and friends can help us interpret the world but they can also color what we see. The same may be true of the influences from various networks that business owners often belong to (ranging from business associations such as Chambers of Commerce, business clubs and so on, to more social links related to, say, sport or leisure activities). And, of course, our own expectations and motivations of what we hope for in life, at work and in terms of a career will affect both judgment and business behavior. The Open University Business Schools (OUBS) has conducted research in this area over the years. The findings from many different entrepreneurial firms, which reveal various influences and feedback loops on the owner-manager's decision-making, are summarized in Illustration 2. Apart from the effects of the various influences that can affect business judgments, the main points to note are:

1. Business situations consist of real challenges, constraints and opportunities that directly impact on the business performance of a firm.

2. However, it is how entrepreneurs perceive these that guide their judgments and actions (which is why accurate market information, the ability to learn and experience are so important).

3. Business perceptions are also influenced by personal and business motivations, peer pressures and cultural influences (it could be argued that entrepreneur's perceptions are more closely aligned with reality).

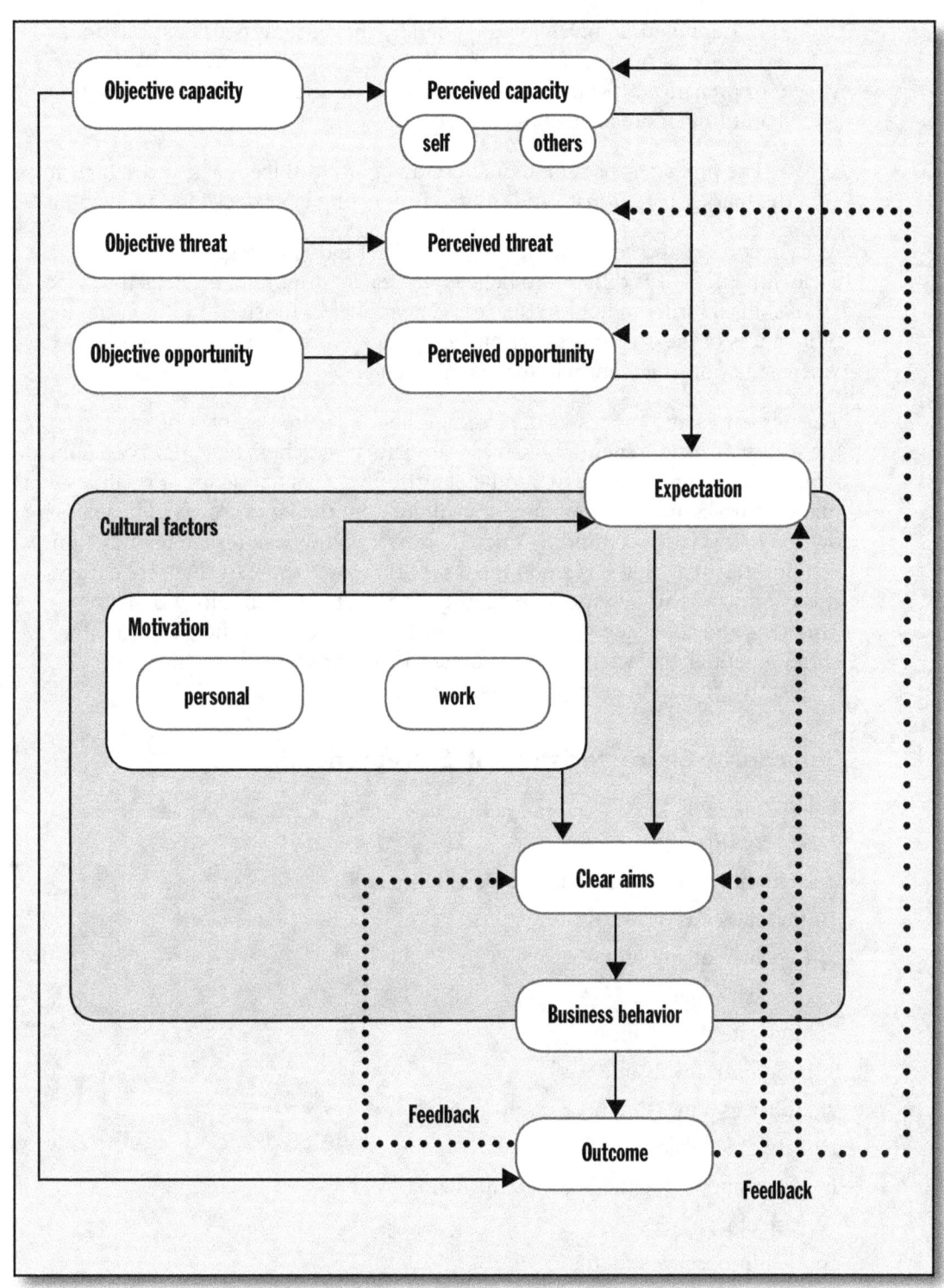

Illustration 2. Model of Entrepreneurial Decision-making

4. Entrepreneurial behavior is guided by the entrepreneur's expectations rather than a rigid set of strategic objectives (again, it may be that the entrepreneur's expectations are more realistic and, maybe, more ambitious than those of other business managers).

5. The process is not static but very dynamic with feedback and signals from the market consciously and indirectly affecting later decisions and actions.

As each context and set of market signals reflect industry, regional and life-cycle influences, it is difficult to believe that each entrepreneur needs the same set of skills in order to achieve success. The model in Illustration 2 reflects the uniqueness of the business situation facing each entrepreneur and the key areas where superior judgment will make a difference.

The influences and processes depicted in the model are complex but so too is the reality of entrepreneurial business. To date, researchers have not been able to identify a core and necessary bundle of attributes, characteristics or qualities that mar out successful entrepreneurs unerringly from the large crowd of business owners. However, a commonly quoted empirical and desk research study of new venture start-ups, that has stood the test of time over the past quarter-century, was conducted through the Massachusetts Institute of Technology by Jeffrey Timmons and colleagues (Timmons et al. 1977). They identified 14 important entrepreneurial characteristics of successful enterprise owners which still frequently crop up in entrepreneurship research.

Behavioral Characteristics of Entrepreneurs

1. Drive and energy
2. Self-confidence
3. High initiative and personal responsibility
4. Internal locus of control
5. Tolerance of ambiguity
6. Low fear of failure
7. Moderate risk taking
8. Long-term involvement
9. Money as a measure not merely an end
10. Use of feedback
11. Continuous pragmatic problem solving
12. Use of resources
13. Self-imposed standards
14. Clear goal setting

Assessment 3. Personal Entrepreneurial Qualities

☐ 1. How many of the entrepreneurial qualities listed above do you feel that already, in the main part, apply to you?

☐ 2. Which ones do you feel a need to find out more about?

☐ 3. Which ones have you already identified as needing more development?

These characteristics appear consistently in other entrepreneurial research studies. For example, more than 20 years ago in a study of Irish entrepreneurs, Cromie and Johns (1983) identified achievement, persistence and self-confidence as general successful business characteristics as well as internal locus of control and commitment to the business, as the characteristics peculiar to entrepreneurs. Some of the qualities that people often find a bit obscure include tolerance of ambiguity (which basically refers to the ability to accept contradictory or unexpected evidence of something while keeping an open mind) and fear of failure (which can lead to pushy, goal-dominated behavior but, in fact, is the opposite of need for achievement – nAch – mentioned in Section 1; the anxiety caused by the fear can sometimes be strong enough to cause the individual to deliberately bring about the failure that is feared). Low fear of failure means that the entrepreneur is prepared to risk things going wrong and can handle setbacks without being deterred (which is associated with but not quite the same thing as high nAch, where failure can lead to severe disappointment and loss of confidence). High achievement motivation is a great driving force but low fear of failure may be very useful in times of business chaos and uncertainty.

Timmons admitted that few entrepreneurs would possess all traits but felt that strengths in one might compensate for weaknesses in others. Many of these characteristics are self-explanatory (such as high personal drive and energy, self-confidence and setting clear goals) and some appear to be linked. Others may be less obvious or well-known, such as money and profits being used as a measure of success compared with others but less as an end in itself. Helping you to develop the last quality in the list, the ability to set clear goals, is the ultimate objective of this unit.

Perhaps a little less familiar is the quality that successful small business owners are said to have – high internal locus of control. This means that they believe that their behavior determines what happens to them and that they can control their own behavior. This is linked to the need for autonomy and personal

Assessment 4. Personal Motivation

☐ 1. Do you feel you are highly motivated to achieve?

☐ 2. Are you competitive and get above average satisfaction from success in non-business areas such as, say sport or academic studies?

☐ 3. Are you able to take setbacks without becoming too discouraged?

There is a tendency for high nAch people to come from very supportive backgrounds and for them to be motivated to achieve in different areas. In contrast, high fear of failure people tend to come from disrupted or non-supportive backgrounds and focus more obsessively on areas where they are more likely to achieve their goals (Kets De Vries 1977) (though they often set goals well below their actual potential in relation to the decision-making model in Figure 2, high fear of failure people would have comparatively low perceived capabilities and expectations whereas high nAch people may be a bit over-confident about their own capabilities and stretch their expectations by setting challenging targets). However, these tendencies are not set in stone and the actual experience of business can have a big effect in inducing either more caution or more confidence. Still, if you are uncertain of your own drive to succeed or your ability to persist, the wisest course of action is to consider pushing your idea as part of a team. Small groups not only provide support, they also have a wider range of abilities and skills and often come up with more considered decisions.

independence expressed by many entrepreneurs as their prime motivation for setting up their own firms (Gray 1998). Internal locus of control has featured fairly consistently in studies on the psychological characteristics of entrepreneurs.

Essentially the concept implies three separate beliefs on the part of individuals that:

1. The outcome of events and situations are susceptible to intervention

2. Individuals can intervene and influence the outcome of situations positively from their perspective

3. They themselves have the skills and capacity to intervene effectively in certain situations or to influence certain events.

The self-confidence, energy flexibility and opportunism associated with entrepreneurial behavior suggests that entrepreneurs are individuals who are accustomed to getting involved and that they expect positive results from their involvement. In other words, they are prepared to expend energy and mental effort because they expect and often receive appropriate or, in their terms, valuable rewards. Also, they are flexible and opportunistic because they believe they have the capacity to become involved across a broad range of situations. Internal locus of control beliefs are essential to the success of self-motivated behavior and form a central core of the entrepreneur's self-concept. However, it is equally clear that entrepreneurs will not be the only people sharing these beliefs.

Most reasonably successful students at all levels realize that their own efforts in studying have a lot to do with passing. Most people for whom sport is more than just an occasional leisure activity know the value of expending their own efforts on training and the importance of self-confidence. And in business, most chief executives and reasonably able mid-level to senior managers will be accustomed to obtaining positive responses from their personal interventions. It seems clear that people who believe that outcomes basically depended on their own behavior and that they can control their own behavior will generally believe that the control of events of importance to them ultimately rested internally in themselves. This is clearly linked to self-confidence and the ability to self-motivate. However, people with internal locus of control beliefs are in the minority. For many people, their lives are deeply affected by the decisions of people in more powerful positions than themselves which, in business, can include strong partners, customers and suppliers (as Porter's five-forces model has identified). Even more pervasive than the belief that powerful others exert a determining control or influence are widespread beliefs that events are determined by chance or luck. Assessment 5 provides you with an opportunity to see where you currently stand (but note that locus of control beliefs are also influenced by context and can vary over time, especially if success breeds success).

These concepts have been found to be useful in analyzing the behavior and beliefs of successful entrepreneurs. If you feel you scored too low for your own liking, this is another indication that a team approach may be best. Indeed, Assessment 5 could also be useful in developing a balanced entrepreneurial team (not everyone can be leader with a firm belief in their ability to control destiny; opportunity often springs from being open to luck and chance happenings and most good teams rely on some members being prepared to follow more powerful others). If you want to boost your feeling of internal locus of control, one suggestion would be to set yourself attainable objectives and push yourself to achieve them. However, it is important to bear in mind that psychological scales and tests of this kind only ever measure tendencies (not absolute and immutable behavior that holds in all circumstances) and never attain anything like 100 percent accuracy. And, in any case, personal belief and motivation is only one part of the entrepreneurial equation.

Assessment 5. Locus of Control

Complete the entrepreneurial attributes "locus of control" questionnaire. This will give you an estimate of your own locus of control belief profile and what dominates – internal, external or chance.

Select one of the three choices, depending on whether you agree or disagree with each statement. (A scoring version is available at:

http://openlearn.open.ac.uk/file.php/3038/!via/oucontent/course/106/ b722b322_1_activity2-2.swf)

Agree Neutral Disagree	To a great extent my life is controlled by accidental happenings.
Agree Neutral Disagree	I feel like what happens in my life is mostly determined by powerful other people.
Agree Neutral Disagree	My own behavior will determine whether I can start my business
Agree Neutral Disagree	When I make plans, I am almost certain to make them work.
Agree Neutral Disagree	Often there is no chance of protecting my personal interests from bad luck.
Agree Neutral Disagree	When I get what I want it's usually because I am lucky
Agree Neutral Disagree	Even if I were a good leader, I would not be made a leader unless I play up to those in positions of power.
Agree Neutral Disagree	I have often found that what is going to happen will happen.
Agree Neutral Disagree	My life is chiefly controlled by powerful others.
Agree Neutral Disagree	People like myself have little chance of protecting our personal interests when they conflict with those of powerful other people.

Agree Neutral Disagree	It's not always wise for me to plan too far ahead because many things turn out to be a matter of good or bad fortune.
Agree Neutral Disagree	Getting what I want means I have to please people above me.
Agree Neutral Disagree	Whether or not I get to implement my ideas depends on whether I am luck enough to be in the right place at the right time
Agree Neutral Disagree	If important people were to decide they didn't like my idea, I won't get off the ground.
Agree Neutral Disagree	I can pretty much determine what will happen in my life.
Agree Neutral Disagree	I am usually able to protect my personal interests.
Agree Neutral Disagree	How soon I can try my ideas depends on other people who have power over me.
Agree Neutral Disagree	When I get what I want, it's usually because I have worked hard for it.
Agree Neutral Disagree	In order to have my plans work, I make sure that they fit in with the desires of people who have power over what goes on.
Agree Neutral Disagree	My life is determined by my own actions.
Agree Neutral Disagree	It is chiefly a matter of fate whether I have a few friends or many friends.

3. Entrepreneurial Work Style

The need for supportive, open and communicative policies, structures and cultures in effective entrepreneurial firms as the optimal crucible for successful innovations comes through very strongly from studies of innovation and successful entrepreneurship. However, the strong internal locus of control of successful entrepreneurs suggests there may be a difficulty in accepting the influence of others, powerful or not. And, the strong need for autonomy does not suggest a personality open to sharing of ideas or knowledge. Indeed, the popular image of a successful entrepreneur can sometimes be that of a determined autocrat who lets nothing stand in the way of success. How can these two conflicting pictures of successful entrepreneurship be reconciled? The answer is that, just as there is no one 'entrepreneurial personality' and people have different styles of learning, so too are there different management and leadership styles that vary between particular entrepreneurs, in their particular firms facing their own particular set of circumstances.

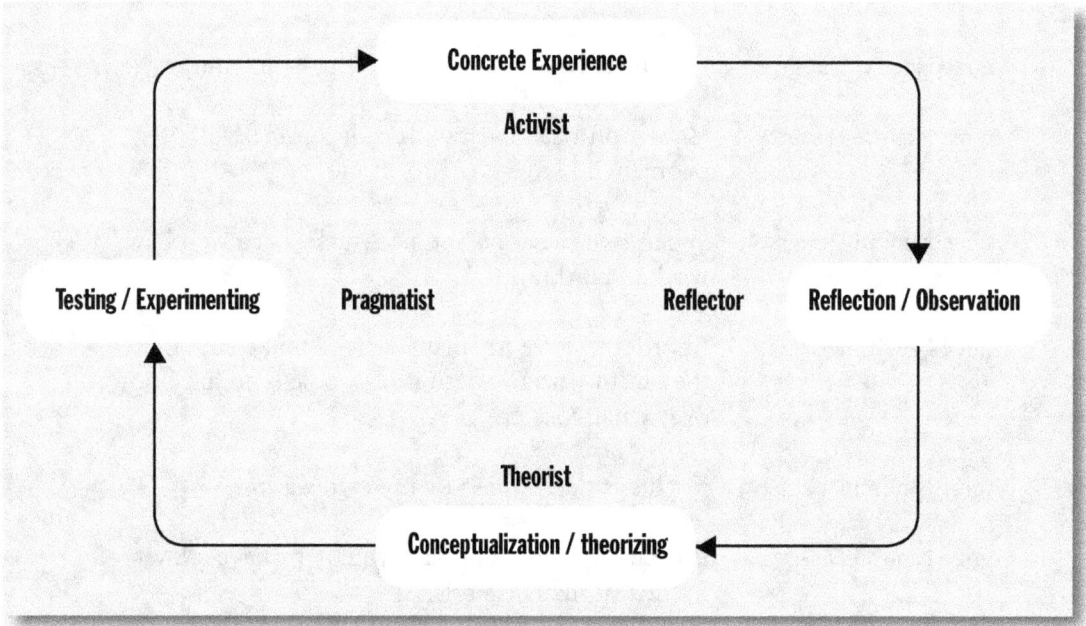

Illustration 3. Experiential Learning Cycle

Looking more closely at learning styles based on the Lewin/Kolb experiential learning cycle (Illustration 3) that underlies this unit, it is likely that individuals will be drawn more strongly to one of the four stages than to others. David Kolb's model (1973) suggests that entrepreneurial success should be mainly determined by the individual's ability to adapt and dominate continual changes in the business environment through exploring new opportunities and learning from past successes and mistakes. In the context of business, the cycle starts with a concrete experience (say, the launch of a new product, landing or losing a major customer, unexpected poor staff performance, a delivery failure, and so on); moves on to the stage of observation and reflection on what has happened and why; then onto making sense of what has happened in the form of a rule or guide for repeating successes or avoiding similar mistakes; and, finally setting up a new situation to test the new insights or rules (thus creating a new experience for the cycle to start again). In practice, Kolb observed that most people display skills along a 'concrete – abstract' dimension and an 'action – reflection' dimension. This suggested to Kolb that there were basically four learning styles (outlined in Illustration 4).

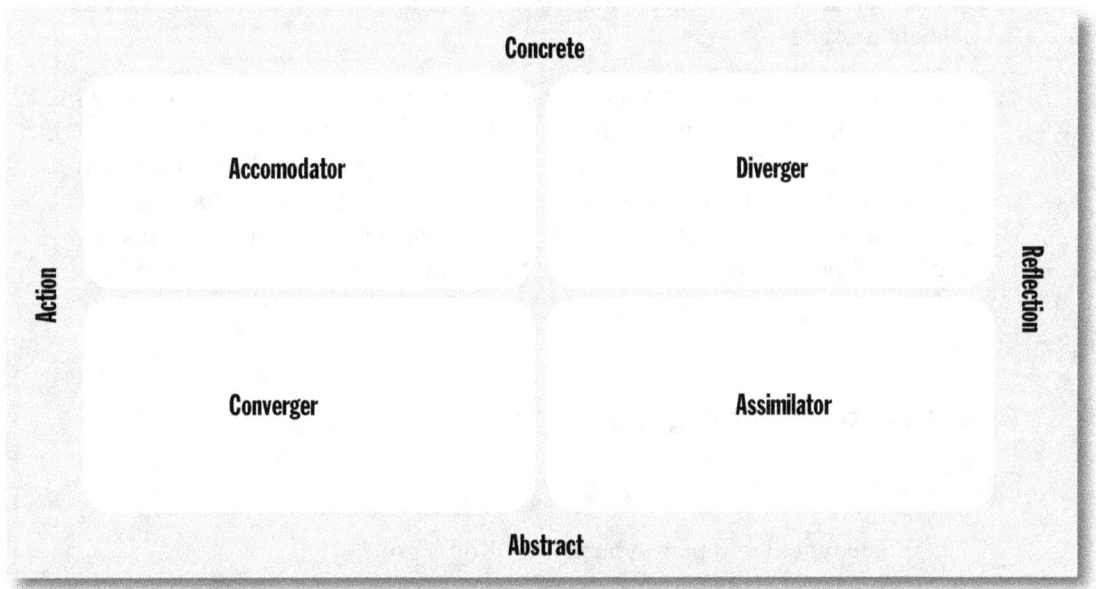

Illustration 4. Kolb's Learning Styles

Following the flow of the cycle, the learning style in upper right quadrant Kolb labeled the diverger. The diverger is able to see concrete experience from different perspectives and to pull different meanings from experience. Kolb saw people who tend to this style of learning as inventive and creative. This could include entrepreneurs in the creative industries such as design and the media. In the lower right quadrant, the assimilator is attracted to creating models and concepts, an approach that would be a strength in consultant and marketing firms. The converger in the lower left quadrant has the learning style that prefers to apply rules and to test them. Kolb saw this as a style that appeals to engineers and technical people. It is also useful in innovations based on R&D. In the final quadrant accommodators are at ease in working with other people. They like to plan and carry out new activities. According to Kolb, accommodators are more prepared to accept risks and this may be the most entrepreneurial learning style.

However, Kolb was at pains to point out that these are not pigeon-holes because people can move from one style to another depending on circumstances or context. Nevertheless, for many people there is a preferred dominant style.

Most definitions of the entrepreneur also stress the ability to organize and combine as the key distinguishing features. This would emphasize the converger's learning style, a conclusion that should find support from influential management writer Peter Drucker (1985). He maintains that innovation no longer results from chance activities but needs to be managed – whether in a big or small firm – as an organized and systematic process. This suggests that preferred learning styles will be directly related to the learning and skills needs perceived at the time and where they work in the enterprise value-cycle. Thus, learning styles are also likely to be linked to preferred management and leadership styles.

Generally, management-orientation can be described in terms of three very broad, but not mutually exclusive areas – structure (organizational and bureaucratic), people (social and motivational) and change (entrepreneurial and innovative) (Ekvall, 1991). Management styles reflect the influences of the management orientation (the requirements of where they manage in the value chain and individual personality). Very broadly, two main categories are often used to

Assessment 6. Learning Styles

☐   1. Which style best reflects your own?

☐   2. Where would you place yourself on Kolb's grid?

☐   3. What sort of balance of learning styles do you think would best fit your needs?

In answering these questions, consider whether you really do think there is a dichotomy between creative thinking and critical thinking. Kolb's categories have been criticized because many people feel that successful managers should have a balance between the two and that, in any case, they are not mutually exclusive. And from our consideration of the characteristics of entrepreneurial firms and the qualities of successful entrepreneurs themselves, the ideal entrepreneurial learning style seems to be one rooted in both action and reflection. Indeed, the fact that business is a social process suggests also that well-developed social skills, such as that of the accommodator, are of prime entrepreneurial importance.

Assessment 7. Management Styles Questionnaire

Complete the Management Styles Questionnaire, noting your score on each of the five styles. Remember, there is no correct answer, only an answer that is right for you. A functioning assessment is available at: http://openlearn.open.ac.uk/file. php/3038/!via/oucontent/course/106/b722b322_1_activity2-3.swf

Management Styles Questionnaire: Management styles – directive or participative? Answer the following twenty questions of this managerial style questionnaire by selecting the button to indicate: if you strongly agree; if you quite agree; if you are undecided; if you quite disagree; or if you strongly disagree. Remember, there is no correct answer, only an answer that is right for you.

Strongly   Strongly
Agree   Disagree

○ ○ ○ ○ ○   I like to be sure that all assignments are clearly defined and logically structured.

○ ○ ○ ○ ○   I am not so concerned about formal organization and authority. I concentrate instead on getting the right people to do the job.

○ ○ ○ ○ ○   I think it is important to have a relaxed atmosphere and not push people too hard.

○ ○ ○ ○ ○   When I promote someone, I think it is important to take into account length of service and the person's economic situation.

○ ○ ○ ○ ○   To be an effective manager you have to keep aloof and not become too friendly with employees.

○ ○ ○ ○ ○   I have succeeded in creating a feeling of pressure to improve personal and group performance continually.

○ ○ ○ ○ ○   I strongly encourage people to try to solve their problems by themselves, even if they make a few mistakes.

○ ○ ○ ○ ○   A lot of my managing is done through informal, friendly conversations that are not scheduled.

○ ○ ○ ○ ○   At least once a week I praise someone personally for doing a good job.

○ ○ ○ ○ ○   I set high standards for performance.

○ ○ ○ ○ ○   I do not rely too heavily on individual judgment; almost everything is double-checked.

Strongly
Agree

Strongly
Disagree

○ ○ ○ ○ ○ I will definitely criticize any employee who makes a mistake.

○ ○ ○ ○ ○ I like to maintain a business-like atmosphere with little socializing or chitchat on the job.

○ ○ ○ ○ ○ There is not much I can do with people who do not have pride in the excellence of their work.

○ ○ ○ ○ ○ I resent employees checking everything with me; if they think they have the right approach they should just go ahead.

○ ○ ○ ○ ○ I reward people in direct relation to the excellence of their performance, and disregard their seniority or whether I like them.

○ ○ ○ ○ ○ I have had to establish quite a few standard practices and procedures to keep the organization orderly and effective.

○ ○ ○ ○ ○ I expect people to check with me before making decisions.

○ ○ ○ ○ ○ I believe a manager should strive for warm, friendly relations with his/her people.

○ ○ ○ ○ ○ I dislike rules and procedures and I eliminate them whenever I can.

Like all tests of this kind, do not look for 100 percent accuracy or a picture of yourself that is set in stone. They often reflect how you feel at the time you do the test. High scores on 'structured' and 'standards' would suggest that you tend to a directive management style while high scores on 'delegative', 'merit' and 'supportive' suggests a more participative management style (of the type recommended for more creative and innovative firms). However, if you have not yet had managerial experience, either in your own firm or working for someone else, it would be interesting to return to the management styles questionnaire after you have had some experience and see if your views have changed. However, there is one more point worth making. To the extent that a test like this can pick up differences in behavioral styles of management, it purports to do so across the board – junior managers, line managers, senior managers and entrepreneurial managers. It is not too difficult to see that any one or a mix of these styles could, in certain circumstances, be suitable for an entrepreneur (even having a structured approach could be essential for entrepreneurs launching a process innovation).

distinguish the main approaches – task-focused and people-focused – and the associated leadership styles contrast directly with participative styles. In fact, a basic two-way classification is far too simple.

The brief discussion above suggests at least five broad management behavioral styles – structured (rules and procedures), delegative (happy for subordinates to take some direct responsibility for their own work) standards (set or agree quality and performance standards), merit (praise and reward good work) and supportive (helpful and enjoy the team's trust). Completing Assessment 7 online will automatically give you scores on each of these styles (with scores around 50 percent representing the average, so that a score of above 60 percent on 'structured' would indicate you like managing by rules or on 'delegative' shows you are comfortable in delegating responsibility).

To get a better understanding of the sort of management style that might be the most suitable for the business that is to launch your idea, we need to go beyond different types of management and look to the role of the entrepreneur as leader. Many managers are mainly administrators or specialists in bounded areas whereas one of the key functions of an entrepreneur is to motivate and coordinate the firm in achieving its goals. Accepting that the main management orientation of the entrepreneur must be to manage change and innovation, in some circumstances this means that the entrepreneur also has to be an extremely efficient manager of the day-to-day challenges of competition while, in other

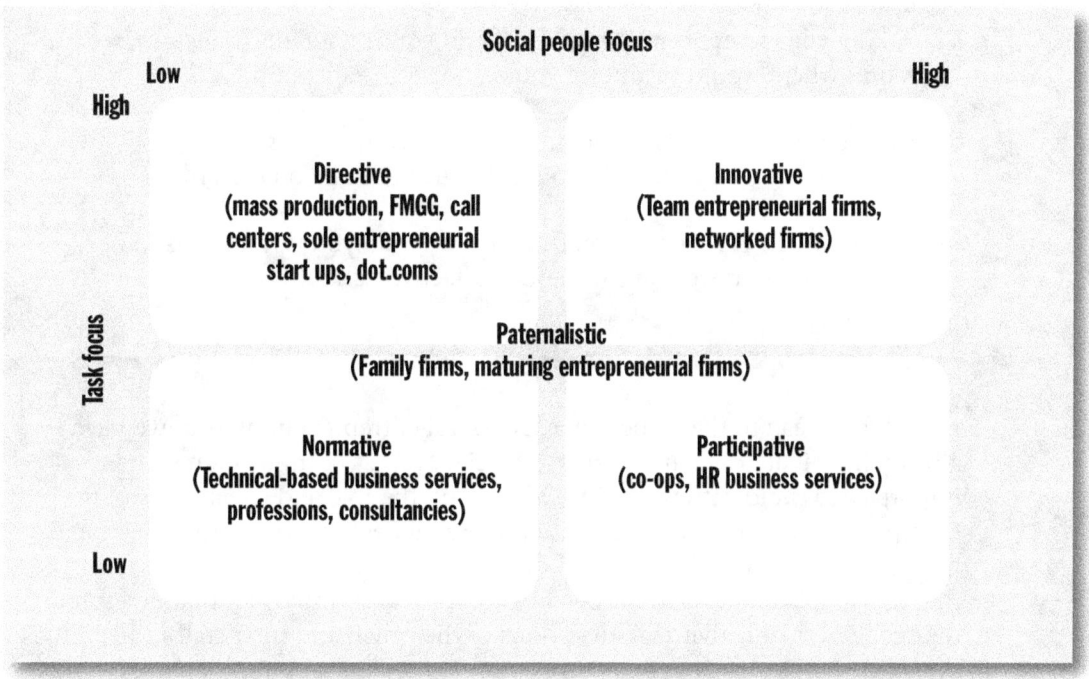

Illustration 5. Leadership Styles

27

cases, administrative functions are delegated and the entrepreneur is required to be an ambassador and leader, with a longer-term perspective. Plotting against the other two management orientations task and people we can identify the five leadership styles as shown in Illustration 5.

The firm that best fits the focus of this course clearly has an innovative leadership style where there is a high focus on both people and tasks. The firm is generally seen as a team and is open to collaborating and sharing with external firms or sources of capabilities. However, research conducted over the years among small firm owners suggest that most like to see themselves in command (especially very small firms with, say, less than ten employees) and having a directive style. Interestingly, growth-oriented small firms that have a history of growth, and slightly larger small firms, are much more likely to see themselves as being 'one happy family' (paternalistic style) or having a participative style. The firms that are governed by external rules and procedures, have a comparatively low people and task focus and generally have a structured management style that does not encourage innovation (though in some professions there can be a strictly limited delegation).

Assessment 8. Leadership Styles

☐ 1. Which leadership style best reflects your own?

☐ 2. Taking your scores on Assessment 7 and your own reflections into account, where would you place yourself on the leadership grid?

☐ 3. Considering the needs of the firm that will launch your entrepreneurial idea, where do you feel you should be on the grid?

☐ 4. If they are different points on the grid, what do you think needs to be done in order to move you to where you feel you should be?

In looking ahead to the launch of a successful entrepreneurial idea, we have already highlighted the importance of social process in innovation so it is important to avoid getting too fixated only on the role and capabilities of the entrepreneur. As Illustration 2 (Entrepreneurial decision-making) in Section 2 implies, it is the overall capacity of firms, real and perceived, rather than just the individual abilities of their owners, managers or employees that determine the scope of their activities. Perceptions of their own and their staff's capabilities plus their perceptions of competitors' capabilities has an important part to play in determining small firm owners' expectations of success. However, there are also likely to be cultural factors of a more general nature which influence perceptions of desired abilities, resources and skills. Entrepreneurs may well be able to identify crucial skills and tasks more accurately than other small business managers. Entrepreneurs can also be defined in terms of their ability to perceive and to respond to these changes more quickly than other business managers. With reasonable feedback, it is relatively straightforward to discuss opportunities and to identify the gaps between reality and perception. However, customer and consumer needs are often ill defined, hidden from view and difficult to quantify Certainly, the perception of many lower level needs (either the needs of entrepreneurs or of customers) are even more strongly determined socially through broad cultural or more immediate occupational influences.

It seems reasonable to hold that effective business judgment reflects the correspondence of an individual's perceived capacities, opportunities and threats to their objective possibilities and the individual's ability competence) to act upon that information (as in Illustration 2). It is not too difficult to then interpret the list of common entrepreneurial behavioral characteristics previously listed in terms of business competence. The successful entrepreneurial firm needs the right balance of competence in the team as a whole rather than seeking them in a single individual. Modern management theory is certainly moving in this direction and away from older hierarchical, scientific management or management-by-objectives models. In reality, your leadership and management styles will be determined by what you feel most comfortable with and what you feel is the norm in the circumstances (but remember that the people you are dealing with also have their feelings about what is a 'normal' management or communications style for the circumstances). By now we shall assume that you have worked out many of these issues to your own satisfaction but, if you need more help, the following activity on teamwork issues may help you consider them more systematically.

Assessment 9 should help you identify both your own capacity for team working as well as areas in which you need to develop or delegate. As well as identifying internal strengths, efficient entrepreneurial firms require financial, physical and technical resources which they are increasingly drawing from external sources, as and when they are needed. In many industries, employment relations are giving way to contractual relations and the main function of core staff becomes servicing customers and ensuring contract compliance. Also, industrialized societies have seen a significant growth in the number of qualifications, regulations and standards that govern commercial life and require particular skills or abilities, often in response to the pressures of global competition. Thus a valuable entrepreneurial capability is having the leadership ability to maintain focus on the ends while at the same time to have the management ability to take into account the needs of the whole firm while addressing the means.

Assessment 9. Teamwork Ability

Complete the Team-working ability checklist below. Consider the last time you worked with or managed a group of at least two other people (preferably but not necessarily one related to business or work). Write a brief 1–2 line description of the group or team. Try to answer the following questions. If the answer is 'Yes', write a brief example. If the answer is definitely 'No', write the main reason.

Yes   No

❏   ❏   **1. Was there a lack of shared common purposes (even if not well articulated?)** Some sense of shared purpose, even if implicit, is one of the defining features of a team. If that doesn't exist the team leader or coordinator needs to develop it or the group never becomes a team.

_____

❏   ❏   **2. Did group members fail to communicate with each other?** For a sense of shared purpose to develop and grow, and for the work of the group to be more than the sum of the work of individual members, frequent and effective communication between members is of paramount importance.

_____

❏   ❏   **3. Were many decisions taken spontaneously without full discussion?** The lack of shared purpose and poor communication means no sense of priorities or direction in discussions, and opinions or intentions expressed by more enthusiastic or articulate members may be accepted without any due consideration, driven more by the strength of individual's immediate feelings rather than in an attempt to achieve some agreed objective.

_____

4. Did some types of people dominate more than others? To be maximally effective as a team, the communication needs to be genuinely two-way and to include all members (and all members need to feel that they have played a part – though it is inevitable that some members become more prominent at any given time due to their experience, expertise, personality, and so on.)

_____

5. Did some group members criticize but fail to participate in the decisions? Feeling left out our pressured into doing something that quicker or more vocal members enthused about often leaves the more thoughtful or cautious members dissatisfied; their dissatisfaction can quickly turn to frustrated criticism but a lack of shared purpose can make it difficult to purpose alternative actions.

_____

6. Did group members seem dissatisfied that their views and strengths were not paid due respect? The points made in relation to question 4 and 5 are relevant here. One effect of a clique emerging that others follow, almost by default, is bound to be frustration and a feeling of marginalization by members whose views are heard. And the lack of shared purpose means that there will be little sense of what skills and knowledge are important.

_____

7. Were members unclear about their own roles or tasks in the group? The lack of roles and tasks that make best use of the capabilities of members is a direct consequence of lack of purpose and poor communication (though in groups with an implicit sense of purpose, there can be a tacit understanding that members with particular sets of skills and knowledge will perform particular tasks – but the dangers of breakdowns in communication remain always high.)

_____

☐   ☐   **8. Did group members exhibit low commitment?** Referring to the points made in questions 5 and 6, people join many types of groups (such as cultural, political, and so on), as well as business organizations or firms, usually for their own reason and with some expectations but, if there is no sense of shared purpose or effective communication of ideas, it is inevitable that their commitment to the group will fall away.

_____

☐   ☐   **9. Did group members lack opportunities to the learn the appropriate skills to participate fully?** A very strong sign that a group actually does have an implicit sense of common purpose that there is a discussion and development of a shared understanding of what members should be able to do and what capabilities are lacking. If these issues are not being discussed, it is unlikely that the group will develop a shared purpose, the essential defining feature of a team.

_____

☐   ☐   **10. Did you personally find it difficult to influence the decisions or discussions of the group?** The other questions referred to behavior of all people in the group of which you were a part. To the extent you identified strengths and weaknesses of the group or team, you were part of that. This question explicitly asks you to reflect on your own role, remembering that the team leader or coordinator is only one among other vital team roles -- such as provider of particular expertise or knowledge, facilitator of discussion and involvement of other members, "the voice of reason or caution", the iconoclast (breaker of conventions and the thinker "outside the box"), and the administrator, the minute keeper, the team's "historian", and so on.

_____

4. Summary

The important points in this introductory document are:

- Defining the entrepreneur in terms of economic function and role.

- Identifying the key characteristics of successful entrepreneurs and entrepreneurial firms.

- Considering the role of entrepreneurial motivation in decision making and business behavior.

- Identifying leadership and management styles appropriate to an entrepreneurial firm

- Considering the entrepreneurial team needed to support your idea.

OTHER OPEN LICENSE RESOURCES ON ENTREPRENEURSHIP

McCubbrey, "Business Fundamentals" (2009), 336 pages.

http://opencollegetextbooks.org/mccubbrey-business-fundamentals-2009/

(License: CC-BY) Excerpt: "The Business Fundamentals text is designed to introduce students, particularly those in developing economies, to the essential concepts of business and other organizations. It does this by focusing on small, entrepreneurial start-ups, and expanding the discussion in each chapter to include issues that are faced in larger organizations when it is appropriate to do so. Traditional business models are discussed as well as eBusiness models, with appropriate links to the IS Global Text and other relevant websites. All major functional areas of modern organizations are covered."

ENTREPRENEURSHIP: GLOSSARY OF TERMS

The following glossary is taken from the U.S. Department of State publication, *Principles of Entrepreneurship*. Some information provided by Jeanne Holden, a freelance writer with expertise in economic issues. She worked as a writer-editor in the U.S. Information Agency for 17 years.

Angel investors: Individuals who have capital that they are willing to risk. Angels are often successful entrepreneurs who invest in emerging entrepreneurial ventures, often as a bridge from the self-funded stage to the point in which a business can attract venture capital.

Assets: Items of value owned by a company and shown on the balance sheet, including cash, equipment, inventory, etc.

Balance sheet: Summary statement of a company's financial position at a given point in time, listing assets as well as liabilities.

Breakeven point: Dollar value of sales that will cover, but not exceed, all of the company's costs, both fixed and variable.

Bridge finance: Short-term finance that is expected to be repaid quickly.

Browser: A computer program that enables users to access and navigate the World Wide Web.

Business incubator: This is a form of mentoring in which workspace, coaching, and support services are provided to entrepreneurs and early-stage businesses at a free or reduced cost.

Business plan: A written document detailing a proposed venture, covering current status, expected needs, and projected results for the enterprise. It contains a thorough analysis of the product or service being offered, the market and competition, the marketing strategy, the operating plan, and the management as well as profit, balance sheet, and cash flow projections.

Capital: Cash or goods used to generate income. For entrepreneurs, capital often refers to the funds and other assets invested in the business venture.

Cash flow: The difference between the company's cash receipts and its cash payments in a given period. It refers to the amount of money actually available to make purchases and pay current bills and obligations.

Cash flow statement: A summary of a company's cash flow over a period of time.

Collateral: An asset pledged as security for a loan.

Copyright: Copyrights protect original creative works of authors, composers, and others. In general, a copyright does not protect the idea itself, but only the form in which it appears – from sound recordings to books, computer programs, or architecture. The owner of copyrighted material has the exclusive right to reproduce the work, prepare derivative works, distribute copies of the work, or perform or display the work publicly.

Corporation: A business form that is an entity legally separate from its owners. Its important features include limited liability, easy transfer of ownership, and unlimited life.

Depreciation: The decrease in the value of assets over their expected life by an accepted accounting method, such as allocating the cost of an asset over the years in which it is used.

E-commerce: The sale of products and services over the Internet.

Entrepreneur: A person who organizes, operates, and assumes the risk for a business venture.

Equity: An ownership interest in a business.

Home-based business: A business, of any size or type, whose primary office is in the owner's home.

Income statement: Also known as a "profit and loss statement," it shows a firm's income and expenses, and the resulting profit or loss over a specified period of time.

Intangible assets: Items of value that have no physical properties, such as ideas.

Intellectual property: A valuable asset for an entrepreneur. It consists of certain intellectual creations by entrepreneurs or their staffs that have commercial value and are given legal property rights. Examples of such creations are a new product and its name, a new method, a new process, a new promotional scheme, and a new design.

Inventory: Finished goods, work in process of manufacture, and raw materials owned by a company.

Joint venture: A legal entity created by two or more businesses joining together to conduct a specific business enterprise with both parties sharing profits and losses.

Liabilities: Debts a business owes, including accounts payable, taxes, bank loans, and other obligations. Short-term liabilities are due within a year, while long-term liabilities are due in a period of time greater than a year.

Limited partnership: A business arrangement in which the day-to-day operations are controlled by one or more general partners and funded by limited or silent partners who are legally responsible for losses based on the amount of their investment.

Line of credit: (1) An arrangement between a bank and a customer specifying the maximum amount of unsecured debt the customer can owe the bank at a given point in time. (2) A limit set by a seller on the amount that a purchaser can buy on credit.

Liquidity: The ability of an asset to be converted to cash as quickly as possible and without any price discount.

Marketing: The process of researching, promoting, selling, and distributing a product or service. Marketing covers a broad range of practices, including advertising, publicity, promotion, pricing, and packaging.

Marketing plan: A document describing a firm's potential customers and a comprehensive strategy to sell them goods and services

Networking: (1) Developing business contacts to form business relationships, increase knowledge, expand a business, or serve the community. (2) Linking computers systems together.

Niche marketing: Identifying and targeting markets not adequately served by competitors.

Outsourcing: The practice of using subcontractors or other businesses, rather than paid employees, for standard services such as accounting, payroll, information technology, advertising, etc.

Partnership: Legal form of business in which two or more persons are co-owners, sharing profits and losses. . Patent: A property right granted to an inventor to exclude others from making, using, offering for sale, or selling an invention for a limited time in exchange for public disclosure of the invention when the patent is granted.

Patents: A patent grants an inventor the right to exclude others from making, using, offering for sale, or selling an invention for a fixed period of time – in most countries, for up to 20 years. When the time period ends, the patent goes into the public domain and anyone may use it.

Small Business Administration (SBA): Created in 1953, it is an independent agency of the U.S. federal government that aids, counsels, assists, and protects the interests of small business.

Small Business Development Centers (SBDC): SBA program using university faculty and others to provide management assistance to current and prospective small business owners.

Service Core of Retired Executives (SCORE): A non-profit organization dedicated to entrepreneurs' education and the success of small business. It is sponsored by the SBA to provide consulting to small businesses.

Seed financing: A relatively small amount of money provided to prove a concept; it may involve product development and market research.

Social entrepreneur: Someone who recognizes a social problem and uses entrepreneurial principles to organize, create, and manage a venture to make social change. Social entrepreneurs often work through non-profit organization and citizen groups, but they may also work in the private or governmental sector. Many successful entrepreneurs, such as Bill Gates of Microsoft, have become social entrepreneurs.

Sole proprietorship: A business form with one owner who is responsible for all of the firm's liabilities.

Start-up financing: Funding provided to companies for use in product development and initial marketing. It is usually funding for firms that have not yet sold their product commercially.

Trademarks: A trademark protects a symbol, word, or design, used individually or in combination, to indicate the source of goods and to distinguish them from goods produced by others. For example, Apple Computer uses a picture of an apple with a bite out of it and the symbol ®, which means registered trademark. A service mark similarly identifies the source of a service. Trademarks and service marks give a business the right to prevent others from using a confusingly similar mark. In most countries, trademarks must be registered to be enforceable and renewed to remain in force. However, they can be renewed endlessly. Consumers use marks to find a specific firm's goods that they see as particularly desirable – for example, Barbie dolls or Toyota automobiles. Unlike copyrights or patents, which expire, many business's trademarks become more valuable over time.

Trade Secrets: Trade secrets consist of knowledge that is kept secret in order to gain an advantage in business. "Customer lists, sources of supply of scarce materials, or sources of supply with faster delivery or lower prices may be trade secrets," explains Joseph S. Iandiorio, the founding partner of Iandiorio and Teska, an intellectual property law firm. "Certainly, secret processes, formulas, techniques, manufacturing know-how, advertising schemes, marketing programs, and business plans can all be protected." Trade secrets are usually protected by contracts and non-disclosure agreements. No other legal form of protection exists. The most famous trade secret is the formula for Coca-Cola, which is more than 100 years old. Trade secrets are valid only if the information has not been revealed. There is no protection against discovery by fair means such as accidental disclosure, reverse engineering, or independent invention.

Unsecured loan: Short-term source of borrowed capital for which the borrower does not pledge any assets as collateral.

Variable costs: Costs that vary as the amount produced or sold varies.

Venture investors: An institution specializing in the provision of large amounts of long-term capital to enterprises with a limited track record but with the expectation of substantial growth. The venture capitalist also may provide varying degrees of managerial and technical expertise.

About Textbook Equity

Textbook Equity, located in the heart of Silicon Valley (Campbell, CA), is a creator, publisher, distributor, and seller of open textbooks for college students. The company's mission is to provide inexpensive open textbooks in print and digital formats as well as support the promotion of open academic resources globally. Using technology and processes that greatly advances the way textbooks are created, produced, and distributed, we find, vet, edit, modularize, enhance, market and sell open textbooks in the top 20 core community college academic disciplines. Sold at low prices or available for free, these textbooks are equivalent to the most popular textbooks in use today.

Textbook Equity, Inc.

View Textbook Equity's repository at opencollegetextbooks.org

www.ingramcontent.com/pod-product-compliance
Lightning Source LLC
Chambersburg PA
CBHW081240170526
45165CB00009B/3135